Are you a Dragonfly?

For Kit—J. A.

For the Ladies of Holsworthy Library—T. H.

KINGFISHER
LONDON & NEW YORK

Copyright © Macmillan Publishers International Ltd 2001
Text copyright © Judy Allen 2002

Published in the United States by Kingfisher,
120 Broadway, New York, NY 10271
Kingfisher is an imprint of Macmillan Children's Books, London.

Distributed in the U.S. and Canada by Macmillan,
120 Broadway, New York, NY 10271

Library of Congress Cataloging-in-Publication Data
Allen, Judy.
Are you a dragonfly?/by Judy Allen; illustrated by Tudor Humphries.—1st ed.
p. cm.—(Backyard books)
1. Dragonflies—Juvenile literature. [1. Dragonflies.] I. Humphries, Tudor, ill. II. Title.
QL520.A44 2001
595.7'33—dc21   00-048815

ISBN 978-0-7534-5805-1

Kingfisher books are available for special promotions and premiums. For details contact:
Special Markets Department, Macmillan, 120 Broadway, New York, NY 10271.

For more information, please visit www.kingfisherbooks.com

Printed in China
20
20TR/1123/WKT/DIG(MA)/128MA

EU representative: 1st Floor, The Liffey Trust Centre,
117-126 Sheriff Street Upper, Dublin 1 D01 YC43

Are you a Dragonfly?

Judy Allen and Tudor Humphries

KINGFISHER
LONDON & NEW YORK

Are you a dragonfly?

If you are, your mother laid
her eggs in the stems
of water plants.

You swam out of one of them—and
so did lots of others just like you.

You are VERY small.

You are very hungry.

And guess what?
You can breathe water
through the end of your tail.

Eat and grow.

Eat tiny water creatures.

6

You have a special grabber for
catching them. It's called a mask
because it covers half your face.

Creep up on your prey—
then shoot out your mask
   and grab it.

Eat and grow
until your skin
is so tight you
have to take it off.

Then eat and grow
some more, and do it again.

8

And again.

And again.

Don't worry, there will always
be new skin underneath.

Now that you
have grown larger,
you can eat larger food.
Try a tadpole or a small fish.

But be careful—there are plenty
who would like to eat YOU.
Beware of water beetles.
Water beetles

pounce!

Beware of ducks.
Ducks dive, and
they're BIG.

Two years have passed. You're bored
with life in the water.

Crawl up a plant stem
into the air.

Do this at night so birds
don't see you and eat you.

Hold on tight. As you dry,
your skin splits one more time.

Slowly, slowly,
climb out
of your
old skin.

First pull
your head free.
Then pull
your legs free.

Flop over backward
and rest.

14

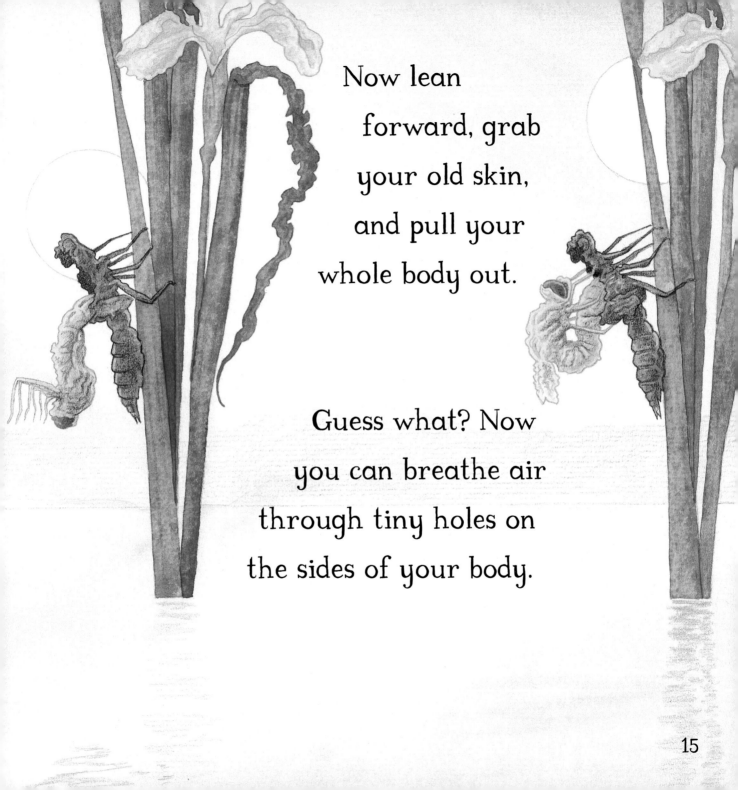

Now lean
forward, grab
your old skin,
and pull your
whole body out.

Guess what? Now
you can breathe air
through tiny holes on
the sides of your body.

You're a dragonfly!

At first you're very
pale and crumpled.

But your beautiful
colors will come, and
your two pairs of wings
will straighten out.

You're a fantastic flyer.

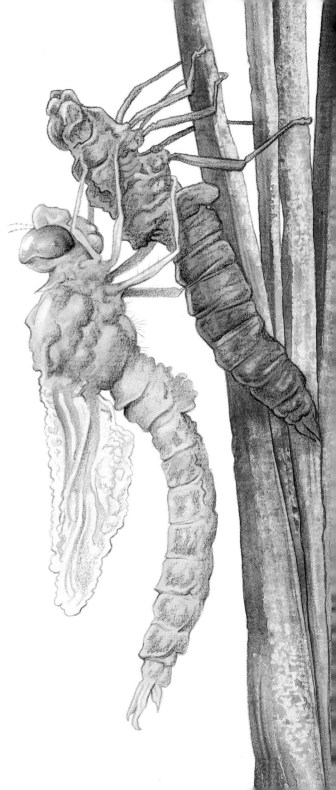

You can fly fast,

you can hover,

you can even fly backward.

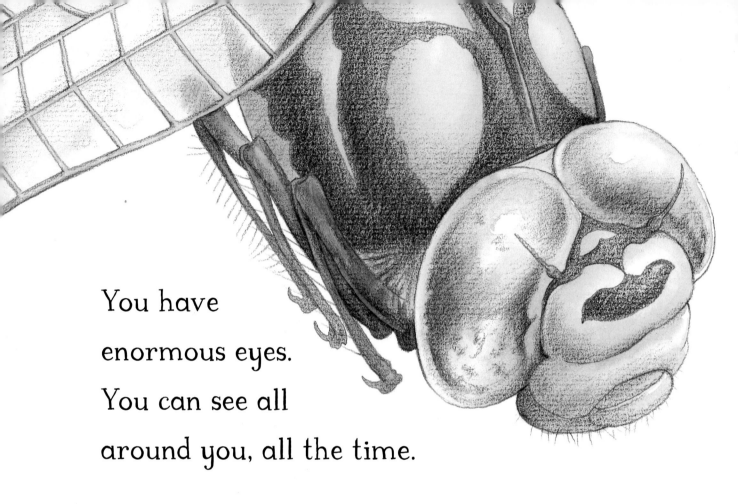

You have
enormous eyes.
You can see all
around you, all the time.

You can see what's behind you,
in front of you, above you,
below you, and beside you.

This is very useful
when you're looking for food.

This is also very useful when
you are dodging hungry birds
and avoiding spider's webs.

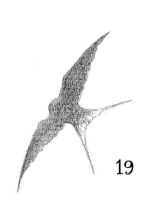

You were a fierce hunter
underwater—now you are
a fierce hunter in the air.

Hunt over ponds and streams
and slow-flowing rivers.
Hunt over marshes
and in forests.

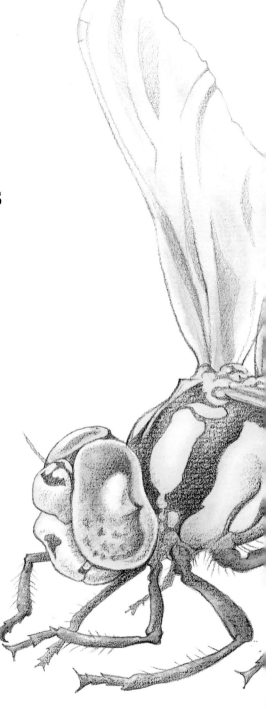

Hold your legs out in front
of you to catch your prey.

Hunt midges and mosquitoes,
flies, wasps, and small butterflies.

When you catch
something, eat it.

You are a hawker—
you hunt while you're flying.

This dragonfly is a darter—it
sits still until it sees its prey, then
it darts out and grabs it.

This is not a dragonfly at all.
It's a damselfly. It's thinner and
lighter and slower than you.
It likes to pick small insects
off leaves and flowers.

Now look around you.
If you and all your friends look
a little like this

or this

or this

you are not a dragonfly.

You are...

...a human child.

You can't fly.

You can't breathe underwater.

It's very unlikely that you have
a mask attached to your face.

But you can do a lot of things
that dragonflies can't do.

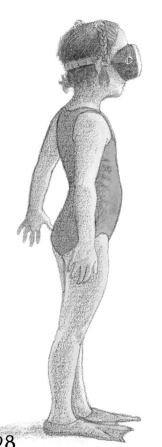

You don't have to keep
taking your skin off, and
you don't have to eat
midges and mosquitoes.

Best of all, you'll
never, ever, EVER
be eaten by a duck.

Did You Know...

... there are around 7,000 different kinds of dragonflies.

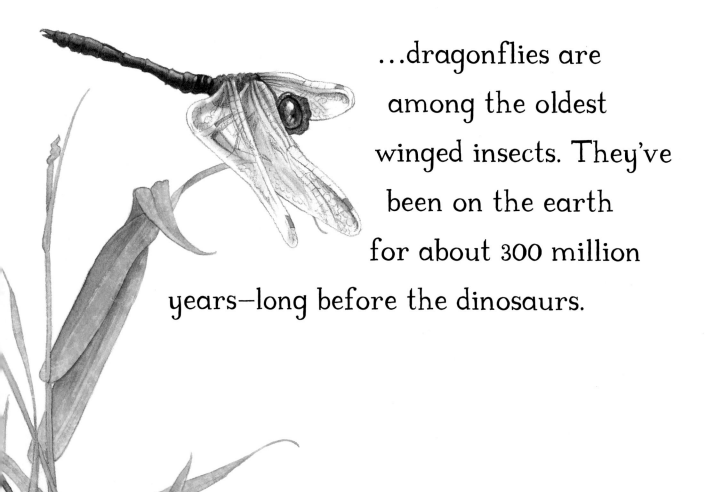

...dragonflies are among the oldest winged insects. They've been on the earth for about 300 million years—long before the dinosaurs.

…dragonflies have two pairs
of wings. They can beat each
pair separately, which is why they
are such great flyers.

…dragonflies usually rest with their
wings spread out, but damselflies usually
fold their wings above their backs,
the way butterflies do.

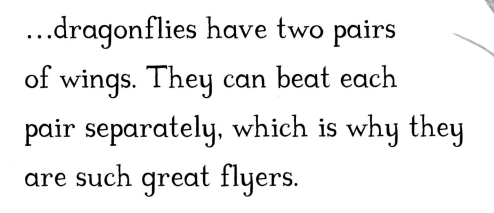